A Chunk

Of

Richness

A Chunk Of Richness

<for short and long term/>

Marcus Lapraxis

The book of Everyone and Nobody

A Chunk Of Richness *<for short and long term/>*

Diagramming: Marcus Lapraxis

© Marcus Lapraxis

All rights reserved

2019

ISBN: 9781097991037

Content

What everyone wants	9
The power of the tangible	12
The path of wealth	18
The new standard of wealth	29
The formula of wealth	44
The awakening of greatness	75
Success programming	79
The wealth programming	84
Being Rich –for short and long term-	112
References	121

A Chunk Of Richness

What everyone wants

If we took a sample of the world's population and conducted a survey and the questions referred to their wishes, in short, all their wishes would be represented by a single word: **SUCCESS.**

Considering that success can be seen as the probability that an event will occur or not, and that happening and not happening are two forms of success, here I refer success as the occurrence of a positive event for all parties involved in the sample that could be taken for purposes of being studied. For example, let's think about a Win-Win relationship. It would be very nice if any event returned welfare to those who provoke it. In a business relationship, it is expected that to be a business, the parties benefit, otherwise, it would not be a business.

Given the above, one could summarize that success is synonymous with winning. I AM SUCCESSFUL IN THE MEANITY IN WHICH I WIN. Being successful is a reference to achieve some goal or purpose. If I achieve my goals, I feel successful.

Success means being successful, then reinforces the idea that someone loses. Consequently, if there are few winners in the world, it could mean that there are many losers. But optimistically, we could say that we are all simply sharing the pizza and that is why we cannot realize that we are also winning. Perhaps it is not seen because it is so little, or because our desires surpass our reality.

The human reality is that from any conglomerate that was taken to be studied and assess their desires, we will see that each member of the sample will always have very high expectations regarding their reality, and therefore it will not be easy for them to notice that they are winning; you will see that you are losing or that you have not reached your goal. This being a common denominator, then we should make a correction to the concept and feeling of success, or to the way of reaching it.

YOU HAVE TO LEARN TO BE SUCCESSFUL. And it seems that it is talking about being happy. Yes, as the formula of happiness. What many sell: HOW TO REACH THE FULL HAPPINESS. They are right. If we do not find a way to be happy, we will live overwhelmed. If we do not find a way to feel successful, we will always see ourselves as failures. Now the meaning of the word success begins to change. We are seeing success as a feeling, referring to it as feeling successful. It seems a call to conformism, as if achieving happiness were synonymous with conformity. TO BE SUCCESSFUL is different from FEELING SUCCESSFUL. Someone could be successful and not feel successful. Someone could feel successful and not be successful. We are facing a contradiction or a paradox.

We have learned to feel, think, and to be happy. We have been educated to assimilate in a different way what happens to us. Or we have not received the same experience to respond in the same way to the situations that are presented to us in the daily life. We have been conditioned and that conditioning is responsible for our different perceptions in front the same event. And when we speak of perception, subjectivity comes up, and if the subjective exists, then it seems that there is no other than educating the source of subjectivity. This source is the human being and the origin is in the brain and everything that comes to it.

11

The power of the tangible

It is not enough with the idea of what you want.
Being able to touch it makes it more powerful.

In my university life I had the occasion when a classmate told me an idea that caught my attention. He did not have much time to have entered the faculty. I had certain more semesters in it. While we were holding a conversation, he said: - "You have to have an amulet". And it showed me something that today I could remember as an Atari or a portable Nintendo. I never had a passion for games, because they caused me stress when I tried to play.

What captured my interest in its expression was form and context. I was thoughtful and today is the day I still remember his idea. And if it continues in my memory, it is because it managed to connect two elements, the abstract (idea) and the concrete (object).

A lot has been said about the fact that it is not the same to imagine something as to be able to touch it. And even if it is not the real object, imagine, touch or see what you want, strengthens the desire to make it real. This applies to all areas of life. And practically it is a call to make more concrete the ideas and/or dreams, for example, to turn them into goals and that these are SMART (Specific, Measurable, Achievable, Realistic, and Timely), that translated are intelligent (Specific, Measurable, Achievable, Realistic, and Timely). This makes our dreams concrete.

Going back to the amulet or whatever could be touched, when we have a living image of what we crave, our motivation remains on. For example, the Nintendo of the mentioned partner had several points of strength. He reminded her of beautiful moments, encouraged him to continue working hard to reach new dreams, and put him in front of himself that after working, he could play. In a sense, an immediate reward was established after reaching part of its goal.

An amulet can also be the direct virtual path to that which you desire. For example, a friend of mine always wanted to go to Paris, which, by the way, is the dream of many people. On one occasion, he went to a store and saw a picture with the Eiffel Tower and the same, a glass holder with classic images of Europe. He decided to buy both objects. The painting put him in front of his desk and the glass next to the computer screen. There was no way to avoid connecting with his dreams and motivators while he was working. Remember that something worked.

Our brain will always be a child. He loves fun. Give him fun and he will also give you results. Put something fun beyond the goal to be achieved and you'll have it in your favor. The images and miniature objects could be allies to your dreams. You want to go to the Eiffel Tower and it's not the time, buy a miniature and put it in your favorite place. You want a Ferrari or a luxury car and it is not yet possible, get a faithful impression of one or toy, but faithful representation and place it where you like. With these steps, you will strengthen your ideas, dreams and goals, and you will be more focused every day on what leads you to the prize.

Unless we have a disease that prevents us from doing it, all human beings, including animals we know, like fun. We all want to have fun at some point during the day, and it is very healthy for our performance and achievement of our goals. Dogs that are trained to look for objects, things, lost people, etc., tend to give a prize after reaching the goal. For example, some dogs were trained to locate mines or bombs in Bosnia and

Herzegovina; the prize of the experts for the canines is to throw a ball to them so that they can look for it and bring it to the master so that it can be thrown again. These animals like that game very much. The same applies to us; we should take a moment for leisure.

Reinforcing the power of the tangible, if you cannot embrace the universe, embrace the earth. If you cannot embrace the earth, go conforming to what you are seeing as you move towards the horizon line. With this we return to the creation of SMART goals and another idea. It is necessary to delimit what we intend to achieve in each stage.

Imagine that you are going to build a house. You own the land and it is wide. You have the materials to build a room with your bathroom and kitchen space. It happens that you want to build your entire house. However, if you use the acquired materials, they only give you to build the first line of blocks and you will not be able to live in such a space for long.

It is necessary to split or divide what you intend to achieve. Establish steps or stages, and devote the necessary energy to each one. This will make it achievable that returns pleasure while you progress, and will reduce the level of stress of each moment. You will live in balance and you will begin to cultivate the gift of patience, a necessary ingredient in being and growing as a rich person.

You have to go savoring the pleasures of wealth without falling into poverty. This seems contradictory, and to eliminate the contradiction, one should understand the philosophy and behavior of the rich.

Imagine that you want to buy a sponge cake, the most expensive of pastries. You could buy it full or a piece of it. If you buy it full, you run out of money for the week, and not only that, you will no longer have money to have a balanced diet during that week, and it will be difficult for you to keep up working only with carbohydrates. If you only buy a slice and eat it as a dessert, you have the opportunity to continue with your balanced diet and working happily, so you can buy back the dessert and enjoy its flavor.

Poverty starts in the brain and ends in the plate. Our philosophy and behavior speak of our wealth. Our behavior is only the act. Our way of thinking is the prelude to wealth. Savoring what is within our reach as we advance to the goal, serves as a motivator to continue working for our dreams. That you go savoring the pleasures of wealth without falling into poverty, means two things: first, go taking samples of the pleasure that the future will have, thus managing to make each exhausted step tangible; second, act with caution, so that it will not be that you stumble all the future to give you an overdose of pleasure, not leaving resources to continue with the achievement of the goal. This is a call to be measured in what you are doing. At the same time, this will forge the attitude and aptitude of the rich person who lives within you.

The tangible is returning pleasure to us as we move forward and simultaneously helps us to continue advancing, and with more impetus, and at the same time the culture of wealth is forged; recognize that everything belongs to everyone and no one, that it is attainable and that there is no reason to be surprised, because both you and I are owners of existing richness and those that are still to be created.

The path of wealth

Pigs do not gain weight alone.
For them to do it, they have to be fed.

The key to wealth lies in doing, and doing forges the culture of the rich. Nobody becomes rich without doing anything. In its broad conceptual spectrum, wealth is nourished by what we do. If we do nothing, we do not quantify or qualify the sense of wealth.

The intellectual wealth is forged with the acquisition of knowledge and experiences of thought. Our intellectual gifts increase as we read. Immediately we are in front a mechanism of acquisition of wealth. If most decisions depended on reading, nobody would have the right to speak if they did not read. The reading culture organizes ideas and thoughts and gives us a broader view of all situations in life. At the same time, it is an ingredient that generates wealth if we use it effectively, although in any case, it always guarantees a better psychic and practical life, constituting part of a person's wealth.

Seeing wealth as the sense of having and maintaining goods that help to maintain a dignified life, the image of the farmers comes to my mind. Imagine one who raises pigs. He will have to feed them daily and, as he does, he will see how they get fat. It observes how the banana peel is converted into muscles and fat, and then this meat is converted into money when it sells the product. It looks like it is saving; each shell becomes a benefit. Sold the pig, use part of the benefits to live (feed, dress, have fun...) and he is probably happy. And so he continues his life, feeding, selling and living. We see that his children begin to help him and increase production, and improve processes, and it also increases the quality of life of everyone involved.

If we observe, the farmer has to wait for the pigs to grow and fatten in order to be sold. You can use supplements to speed up the process, but you cannot exceed the time of cell division offered by the pig. In short, you will have to wait, and this will require patience.

Piglets are seen as the symbol of saving. It is an image that comes to us when we want to save, meaning that the more frequent or recurrent our savings, the more our profits will grow. In that the saving is summarized. Saving is a way to increase our capital over time. This would be a classic and passive rich option, which had a capital at a time and decided to save it and live on the interests. The rich modern and active, invest their capital in assets or projects that move the benefits fast, grow fast and maintain stability.

If you do not feed them, they do not get fat. Whatever you want to grow, it will be necessary to be nurtured (your thoughts, your capital, your relationships, everything). Cause and effect are the sense of wealth. After doing what is necessary to reach it, wait, have patience and not skip steps, are the guarantee that one day it belongs to you.

The adventures, adventures are. Anything else is chance. Try to take accurate steps on the road to wealth. You have to do culture while walking, always be aware of the steps taken and their consequences, write down the failures and successes to improve the next action; go creating your model or wealth equation. You have to be reflective.

If chance visits you and you get rich, then do not rush and start studying how rich people became rich in a solid way, because solid wealth comes from a culture that is based on time and that becomes a style of lifetime.

Wealth is a lifestyle that is consecrated in thought, word and deed. Hence it is not so easy to be rich for a few, and even those who reach their material wealth by chance, could end up being rejected by the solid rich, because right now these newbie do not have the pillars of the classic or modern rich.

The authentic rich is reflective, he projects tranquility, he is cautious, he measures the scope of his actions, he enjoys with measure the success of his exploits, he is attentive to changes. Think and act according to what is and controls what is not. It is a domesticated wolf. The wolf is born, it is transformed, but it dies being what it is.

The rich man is a hunter. He knows and recognizes his own traps. The authentic rich is not surprised by the impression of things. He knows that it is the same thing he would do to capture those who love to own luxuries without measuring their possibilities. He knows how to put the bait to attract his possible prey. Know the passions of the poor.

Wealth is an art that is cultivated and learned. Many do not reach it, because all cultivation requires time, and time presses the passions and kills them. Here you have therefore the importance of patience on the road to wealth.

Wealth requires humility. With it we can recognize our limitations and lead us to enjoy the small achievements and thus feel that it is worthwhile to continue fighting for the achievement of goals. If we do not have this ingredient, we end up frustrating and without reaching the goal.

The path to wealth is more the education of the spirit than what is available on a material level. A gold ingot is not educated; the one who owns it is educated. Wealth is more a matter of attitudes than of tangible elements. It's the way we react to assets, what projects us as rich or poor. For this reason, those rich in money are denigrated, those who obtained material goods because right now they won the lottery -for example-, given the high probability that they will lose everything overnight, because wealth requires attitudes that are forged in time.

People who grow up in an environment with wealth are more likely to keep and remain rich. This is because they learn it and assimilate the culture of wealth. The rich millenarians have transferred to the following generations both material things and their culture, and more weight has had the custom than the material, because being rich is a way of life.

Whoever it has something material and perhaps excessively and boasts about it, easily ends up betrayed by its intangible deficiencies, the culture of the rich.

Unfortunately, if a poor man wanted to be rich, he would first have to mold his spirit. The first wealth should be the intellectual; prepare the mind to dominate the concrete world; master the passions. Wealth begins in the mind and ends in appearance.

The authentic rich are simplistic, simple. Use what is necessary. They are practical; use what makes it efficient and effective in their objectives. The more appearance exists, greater deficiencies and greater propensity to fail or to leave the circle of the rich. They who enjoy wealth use what adds to their capital. If you buy an expensive item, you will always do so when you can use it for a longer period of time, which it is of quality, and a sustainable expense and/or investment.

Wealth requires self-control. This ingredient can be found in emotional intelligence. Sadly, the poor find it difficult to control themselves in the situations that dominate their emotions. The rich have to be cold, calculating, and visionary; never stop seeing the negative impact of their actions. Imagine a compulsive buyer. It would be difficult to assimilate him as rich.

In whatever the social class, the principle of conservation should prevail. Classes are not canceled. It is common to hear the expression: "Colleagues do not step on the shoes". Each class must fight for its conservation. The rich man tries to keep his circle; maintains constructive relationships with theirs.

Sometimes, individuals who have not reached wealth, end up damaging their class or family for wanting to please the rich and take a part and perhaps take a leap of grace towards wealth, but fail in the attempt or if they succeed, hard little his glory, because they never belonged to that group, falling by their own weight.

Wealth requires cohesion among the members of the class. Do not damage the base of wealth, the family. The riches are preserved by the existence of a protective core, the family. Riches are transformed by family transfer. You cannot lose this ingredient.

In the family, the base and culture of wealth are felt. And such is the case that those who disengage in family life, end up being poor or unsuccessful. Those who fail, do so for not assimilating the culture of the rich, ending up thinking and acting like the poor. They do not control their passions, they waste, and psychically they do not count on the attitudes and aptitudes of the cultural life of wealth.

It would seem that being poor is bad, but here poor is not the one we know, poor is the one who suffers from wealth, and wealth is a quality that begins in the mind and ends in the act.

Whenever we think of a world of the rich, we think of Europe and perhaps North America. This should lead us to reflect and think about why they are rich. If we go to the United Kingdom, we will see that there reside the first cultures that fought for the conquest of land and property, noting that in time these human groups have achieved an equitable distribution of wealth, that is, they apparently defended the welfare common and gave their blood in bloody battles, defending the villager value with their lives. They did not hesitate to fight for their class and they achieved good for all.

In the culture of the rich there is a paradoxical ingredient, attachment and detachment. The rich will value the riches while he lives, but at the same time he understands that one day he will not be and that his assets will remain with his family. Hence, he understands that he must prepare the offspring so that he can administer what he leaves and perpetuate his lineage. The rich recognizes that the relay technique must be used even in life if necessary, to guarantee the survival of its nucleus.

In the perpetuation of lineage, honor and respect come together in this culture of wealth. We have the rich man who has the responsibility to preserve his history out of respect and honor to his ancestors. This helps him to conserve himself in time and to exalt his existential pride. Real families and millennial families are examples of this type of rich. However, we are talking about the same rich, because wealth requires respect and honor to the causal past. These two qualities are summarized in gratitude.

He who enjoys wealth is grateful, and his best way of thanking is to maintain and multiply what he has received. With this comes to mind the parable of the talents that appears in the Christian Bible. Poor was the one who decided to save the talent because it was only one, and rich, who decided to multiply what he received.

The culture of the rich is as powerful as the yeast in the wheat. It will grow or multiply everything that comes into your hands. It is fertile land. There is no time to see the negative parts to prevent doing what you have to do. The rich man goes ahead with what he receives. The rich man is an innate entrepreneur.

The rich cultivate optimism in the face of adversity. Find the opportunity in the failures. Do not go looking for excuses. Use the ash as fertilizer if that was what was left of their venture. The rich man is the presence of God on Earth.

Because time clouds the past and a price has wealth, the rich must try to be kind as much as possible, because wealth is preserved by the existence of all. Do not hurt the one who supports your riches.

The path of wealth is not traveled overnight. It starts in the mind and transcends life itself.

Everything that you crave, you will have to feed it with thought, word and deed that will lead you to it. Wealth is a way of life. It is cultivated and maintained over time. Being rich is a decision that starts with a thought and transforms everything around you.

The new standard of wealth

Not all that glitters is gold.
The mirrors also shine.

Wealth, defined as a state of satisfaction, should be the only idea left in the current generation. So general that we do not know what it is, and so ambiguous that we prefer not to think about it.

Technology came to narrow the gap and tear down borders. In its initial impact, we were all very motivated by the effect. Those who had never known more closely other cultures, began to get in touch through social networks, and projected some joy to know. For the false conceptions or ideas of rich nations, they opened their eyes to the respect of the lifestyle, and for the reality of truly rich nations, they began to increase their expectations and stop the pushing force.

It happens that with the approach of cultures, many events can be generated; so many that we still cannot measure their consequences. The only thing we can say at the moment is that we are a global village, and having the world in our hands now is a burden that we still do not know how to handle. With the fact of globalization, many concepts collapse and others move. Talking about wealth in a global environment is something that changes the vision of global nations.

Although globalization has been good, it will also be necessary to develop existential defense mechanisms at the psychological level so as not to end up drowned without crossing the river. Its impact has been such that it has affected all areas of human activity and its way of seeing life and the world. Being rich in this new society will have as many implications as being happy.

Now more than ever, the awakening of the authentic rich is necessary, a being that depends less on material reality to continue calling himself rich.

On one occasion it was said that what makes an individual poor is to have such high expectations, that he ends up frustrated; desire so many things, that it moves away from reality. If the current conventional rich human being decides to compete against the world, he is likely to end up exploited in the attempt. Hence, new strategies have to be developed to be able to compete and be preserved.

In developing societies, where there is social inequality, the rich have already had their impact facing the world. They realized that they are not as rich as they thought, and that they turn out to be poor with respect to the world, both in material and intangible terms. This means that they have to activate new ways to remain calm and not be overwhelmed by external demand to preserve their status quo. Here comes emotional intelligence to be a defensive response to the global bombing of nations that have historically been rich.

Now we need a rich, wealthy person who must develop intellectually and emotionally in addition to having his material wealth, because suddenly he could end up as a failure in the attempt to fill expectations that may not correspond to satisfy as rich.

The most interesting thing about being rich is that you cannot depend only on material things. Enriching the intellectual or psychological capacities, become the ally of the new global rich. The current wealth becomes more intangible and leads the human being to have a higher vision of what life and its meaning represent. The purposes begin to change. Intelligently, because right now it could be very difficult to compete in material terms, sharing is more prudent and enjoyable. We go from the value for the material to the value for the cultural. Now we want to discover the cultures of the different nations.

Popular slang shouts that it is not rich who has more, but who less needs, that what makes us happy is not having, but wanting more than we can make reality. Apparently, the poor man wants a lot and makes little possible; he has expectations so high that he cannot reach them. Now we have to help the rich not to become poor in front their approach with other nations. It is necessary to simplify the wealth model, returning to its roots.

If nations are compared against them, they will be able to recognize and corroborate that they are still the same nations, which may remain rich or poor as before. Consequently, although today we call them villages to speak of a tribal model or of global nations, they remain the same. Then there is no need to worry. This is the step ONE, increasing our self-esteem as global nations.

If we see the approach that causes globalization as an effect that enriches our experience as human beings and makes us improve our general vision of life and its meaning, then it is a positive aspect. We might feel that we are not alone, that there are other people who want similar and good things for the world. This is the step TWO increasing our feeling of support as global nations.

If we consider the narrowing of distances and the elimination of borders as an opportunity to learn new techniques to do everyday things and improve our daily practice, then we would be growing or surpassing ourselves, instead of thinking or considering ourselves inferior. This is the step THREE improving our personal and productive attitudes as global nations.

In my Disposable Human Treatise, in Staying Creative, I suggest that coming into contact with new cultures or exposing oneself to them makes us improve our creativity and increase our motivation in life. A global society, where it goes from being a nation to being a village, we all face each other and discover or learn things that we would only learn if we visited the nation that possessed what to learn. Exposing ourselves to cultures, makes us more creative, and this is the step FOUR, improving creativity as global nations.

In a certain sense, sometimes, things happen without planning and we have only to learn from them and grow. The natural thing is that cultures meet in time. Animals have always migrated looking for new opportunities to find food. Human beings have not been alien to such behavior or reality. With adaptive capacity, we will be able to respond to demands and successfully exit what we have created.

Not to lose that which characterizes the rich. He will have to change the focus of his wealth; look out when convenient and stay focused on his local reality when he decides to compete, because first comes first. You cannot pretend to compete against the world when you are not yet competent in your local reality. If you keep trying to improve in your immediate reality, you will have energy to achieve it, because you know that reality better, while if you face the other global nations, you will have to know them thoroughly to compete and win. This is a call to create achievable goals (SMART), lest you end up covering a lot and squeezing a little, paying honor to the poor.

The new standard of wealth requires more intelligent responses to global situations. It requires a rich more focused and clear of what he really wants. You will have to divide to overcome, but not divide groups, divide your goals into goals or establish mental barriers between what matters and does not matter to remain that you are. You must live your own reality, because the rich man is realistic. If you leave reality while moving forward in life, you will end up losing everything. Globalization reaffirms the true meaning of wealth.

The new rich will be those who know how to take part in the global cake and enjoy it because they and others are having access to the cake. The freelance activity, which could become a culture, to represent a way to generate wealth and that requires certain attitudes to face the world I see it as an approximation of the concept of the new rich, where simplification is a vital ingredient.

The new rich will be dual, sedentary and nomadic at the same time. It can be anywhere. Intelligent electronic equipment will be enough to make riches. He will be freer and compete against the world, having to develop skills that he never imagined to be developing.

The new standard of wealth will demand an adequate management of stress and anxiety levels. The new rich will have to effectively manage the pressure and concerns that globalization will permeate in their daily lives. He will have to increase his space for contemplation and reflection. You will have to fight to keep happiness. It will be necessary to soften expectations and not lose sight of leisure time, which is necessary to maintain balance.

In today's generation of the rich, it will have to increase spiritual wealth so that they can survive the bombardment of global interaction. The emotional load is greater when the reference parameters change. Previously, our reference was our local reality. Currently, any decision to make, must consider the global reality or global nations to increase their success rate.

When referring to global nations, I cover the countries that have been approached either by technology or by commercial exchange under a bilateral agreement. In fact, globalization has not been an event that has happened overnight; it has been a natural process carried out by humans since its inception and the invention of writing, but it begins to take shape with the dissemination of knowledge of peoples through printed documents, which are achieved with the invention of the printing press modern for about 1450. This globalization is notorious with the beginning of the conquest and colonization of many regions of the world for 1492.

Although commercial exchange represents the reason for interaction in the initial phases of globalization, electronic communication is what makes it possible to speak of a global village, because it is not just an economic impact. Globalization implies starting to feel what other peoples feel, we begin to see ourselves as one, as a tribe. For example, World War II separated peoples, but united minds and souls before a common cause. When we thought about the explosion of the atomic bomb in Hiroshima in 1945, we were joined by a panic before a possible threat or extermination of humanity. When we watch movies from the Second World War, we relive experiences that although we were not part of them, we felt them as if they had been lived by ourselves, because we are no longer isolated societies. The transformation of forms of communication brings us closer as human beings and global leaders.

The current rich new have many challenges ahead. Facing globalization is the first challenge. Recognize how this economic, social, political, cultural, technological, and business process transform their ways of doing, not being able to leave aside the global aspect to their decisions. Knowing is the second challenge. It cannot act with traditional schemes. If it is an entrepreneur, the most likely is that you have to diversify and better organize your structure or workforce.

It might seem that globalization is a negative phenomenon; however, in terms of competitiveness, although it is difficult for those who do not have the appropriate infrastructure to compete, it will be at the same time their starting motor to update and put themselves at the forefront.

If intelligence consists of giving answers to situations at the right time and in the appropriate way, then the new rich has more opportunities to respond to the demands of the environment. Globalization could be your ally.

A current entrepreneur could make his operations more efficient in the market, increasing his competitiveness; specializing or further defining its niche in the market. He could respond better to the fluctuations of local economies, because it no longer has to be limited to the local, that is, it can also have its company online (online, web), so that there will be a permanent global active market, which will allow him to stay afloat. This will be achieved because barriers to entry to international markets (labor, financial, goods and services market ...) have been eliminated. He has the technologies in his favor. The potential benefits of the new rich are greater at the moment.

As not everything that shines is gold, there are also challenges or impacts that must be faced by the rich. It is not only that the rich ends up being poor with respect to the scale of global wealth, it is that, really, globalization has those risks and can take the existing rich even from its local scale.

Free trade can boost economies, but at the same time it can become a black hole, draining the wealth of less affluent people, because they are at a competitive disadvantage, because their production capacity or generating assets is less than the members of the global market, because right now their policies are not strong enough to reach a point of equilibrium.

With free trade agreements, countries with limited production machinery carry a heavy burden to compete, passing these to an economic model of consumption, because now the foreign offer is greater than what they can offer even at the local level, their supply satisfaction to the internal demand being outdated, preferring to consume what the most powerful nations can produce. Hence, local markets may fall and the entrepreneur ceases to perceive the benefits he obtained before globalization. In a certain sense, it seems that the rich man becomes richer and the poor poorer; here is the economic imbalance.

The current rich of emerging economies, is forced to reinvent him to avoid seeing how his capital is drained by the new economy, the world market economy.

The facilities of access to consumer goods, the possible fall in prices due to the effect of globalization, are the double-edged weapons available to us. To the poor, in terms of economic income, it has been made easier for them to acquire goods that once were more possible for the rich. The rich also enjoy more of the facility, given the generalized liberalization. The sharpest edge of access to mass consumption is consumer financial education.

The deliberate consumption of the masses, including the rich, puts anyone who is driven by impulses to the test. Anyone who falls into the trap of consumerism, of created needs, will end up becoming anything but rich. When the active-passive relationship is lost, any chance of success is lost. Hence, it is necessary to educate the consumer and the rich, so that now they do not end up with a lot of liabilities in their financial lives.

Without delving much, regardless of the visible changes that humanity has always suffered, everything is summarized in a human problem, therefore the fact that always have to end correcting the source of error, the human being. The changes begin with you, with me.

The new wealth banner merits more financial and emotional education. Educate the passions to improve finances. Likewise, the new rich will have to empower themselves of the technologies and the knowledge of the juridical order in front the effects of the globalization, so that it can take profit of the advantages offered and make more coherent decisions with a high probability of success.

The new rich must increase attention to detail, because now their opportunities will be more in the details. This will lead you to specialize to trap or create your niche market. You will have to go out of the conventional and enter into the delivery of supply of needs that perhaps you will be forced or motivated to create.

The current rich will have to be a specialized hunter. He will be forced to know more about psychology and sociology in order to keep his source of income generation afloat. You will have to learn more about emotional intelligence, consumer behavior.

The new standard of wealth does not displace the basic qualities of the classic rich. On the contrary, the fundamental characteristics of the rich must be complemented and strengthened. For example, simplifying will be more necessary in a world with such complex fluctuations.

Riches are there and for everyone. The smartest will know how to drive them to their capital. Here is the need to study the behavior of both competition and the market. More than ever, patience will be necessary for anyone who wants to stay rich or who wants to reach wealth.

Not all that glitters is gold. The mirrors also shine. Do not get carried away by the impression. Just as in the local markets there are deceptions, when we face a global market, the rate of deception may increase, because the political and legal regularizations are not yet so controlled. Access to markets where international jurisdictions have no reach, is something that calls into question any operation that wishes to be done, because security is low. For example, shopping online, where you have no choice but to deposit in an international account, which you can not pursue its owner, because right now there are no legal aspects that would protect you in case of fraud. Web stores could give you interesting offers, but you'll have to be careful about what you want to acquire, the reliability and reputation of the site, the payment options, the support of such options, and so on.

You must be careful with the impressions of the offers. You will have to be more cold and calculating when making decisions.

It is decisions that make you rich or poor. Behind every decision there is a rich man or a poor man.

The formula of wealth

The magic of wealth is in giving.
Add value to the raw material.

Without exaggerating, I dare to say that the first indications of the sense of wealth actions, to which I am going to exemplify, go back to the year 24,000 b.C. and maybe much sooner. Modern terms to refer to wealth, involve adding value to the raw material to receive a benefit for the final product. For the aforementioned time, man already made animal, human figurines and any other type of representation that would be useful to his interests; these were made of clay, which we also know as mud. Whoever practiced this activity, we call him a potter, this one being the example of rich mind that I quote.

The potter adds value to the earth. Turn mud into art or utensil. Clearly, it adds value to that which lacks appreciable form. And that's what wealth consists of, adding value to a thing so that it returns us a benefit in time and offers a utility to the consumer.

The formula of wealth consists of giving, adding value to the raw material. As we add value to the object, if it is, we increase the utility (interest, profit). When you create a product, for example, clay, you give your time and add your creativity; At that time and creativity you put a sale price that includes the purchase price or material expenses. By selling it, you get the capital plus the profit and you keep making and selling the product. As time goes by, a fraction or part of the profits are left as possible savings, which you can keep as such or move to capital to continue increasing your production or to venture into the development of new products. This dynamic keeps you in time and is what I call the natural rate of growth of wealth.

Going back to the potter, we always have to be vigilant to add value to what we do. Nobody is oblivious to this. In natural way, we do it by own motivation. In forced mode, we will do it to respond to the emergence of competition and the need to differentiate in the market.

The current companies remain in a constant dynamism, adding both tangible and intangible value to their products or services; improving customer service, production mechanisms, transportation, global positioning, among countless other variables, to survive or exist in the market. The competitiveness is the day to day.

Capital and profit are the basis of wealth. You can achieve them like the potter, but you can also achieve this by investing in the potter to expand, increase or improve your production, and receive an interest in the money you provide as capital to achieve your goals. You can send the investment through multiple channels, including: direct or indirect.

Within the above options, you can create or develop a product or service, market it and generate your utility. Equally, you can use your capital and approach a producer and invest in your business in exchange for an interest for your money, and you can also associate in case you accept and obtain a portion of your shares. These would be direct ways to generate utility. The magic of this model is in increasing sales to increase net profits. Behind the results, the members of the business will make multiple operational and administrative maneuvers to achieve the purposes of the company. This is to have your company and push it forward with your commitment and all the strategies that could occur or coined by other entrepreneurs or experienced entrepreneurs.

If you are interested in only seeing the final product, then investing in the stock markets is your option. This can be achieved through organized financial markets (stock exchange), unorganized or over-the-counter financial markets, using financial mediators, among other indirect options to generate profits.

The most conventional way to generate profit is banking savings; you take your money and take it to a bank, which usually offers you a utility or annual interest on your saved capital. In this case, the bank serves as the administrator of your money; it lends it under legal terms to a third party, at a profitable interest rate, and returns part of the profit according to the fixed times of capitalization.

Whatever the chosen model, all these lie on the same concept, interest on investment capital.

It might seem strange to tell you that wealth is based on the interest generated by the capital invested or saved, but that is the case. Time is the other variable of wealth. That is why we see that the solid rich have not emerged overnight. The capital increases with time and the frequency with which it capitalizes.

When we decide to invest, among other variables, we take into account the financial return or ROE (Return on Equity) and investment risk. The first one represents the financial performance, which will be the percentage proportion that you will receive in exchange for your capital; this is the interest rate at which the amount is received. The second implies the probability that the yield or benefit is lower than the expected value.

When we venture to invest, we realize that the investments with higher yield waiting tend to have a greater risk involved. Among the variables that affect or compose the risk, there are: credit risk, inflation, currency exchange, among others.

Saving your money in a commercial bank will give you a return below most of the options available in the market. However, the risk of losing or ceasing to perceive what is expected is lesser.

The investing in federal banks, acquiring some treasury bill, offers you a low risk in the short term, because there is support from government funds, thus having legal security. The profitability is good and could be higher than that of commercial banks, associations and cooperatives.

On the other hand, we have the purchase of shares, which have a higher volatility than the price of the bonds.

If we compare an investment in a bank deposit versus the same investment in the stock market, we can observe how the banking curve will be stable and growing in the same time or period while the curve in the stock market will be quite changeable or unpredictable, being able to maintain fairly high peaks, but sudden falls; hence, the behavior of the investment must be constantly monitored.

If investing in the stock market requires surveillance or intelligent systems that warn or alert about changes, investing in another emerging model like the crypto currencies, demands it even more, due to its high volatility. A few have been lucky, they knew when to invest and when to withdraw or sell their shares or crypto currencies. Others have lost a lot in their attempt.

After all, the important thing is that you know that there are multiple options for investment and that you are aware of the risks involved. In the end, your chance of success or failure will be in your dedication, discipline and learning in the market in which you have decided to develop. Here is the cultivation of the art of being in business or in any productive area.

The following equation shows with simplicity the return of an investment.

$$ROE = \frac{Net\ profit}{Invested\ amount}$$

If you invest $ 100 dollars in the elaboration of a product that will be sold for $120 dollars, and of the $ 20 that returns the sale you receive $10 dollars, then the return of your investment has been 10%, that is, 0.10x100 = 10%.

$$ROE = \frac{\$10}{\$100} = 0.10$$

Imagine that you decide not to keep the $10 dollars and only keep $5 and reinvest or add $5 to the initial capital, now your capital is $105 dollars. It happens that the manufacturer and merchant of the product took a week to have the product ready for sale and another week, to sell it. As a result you took 15 days to earn $5 dollars. Smartly, the merchant also decided to add $5 dollars to the production capital, which together with the $5 dollars of yours has increased the base capital to $110 dollars. The manufacturer decides to make the product again with the cost of production and commercialization of $100 dollars; they are left over $10 dollars and he decides to position your product on a web page, where the day after having finished it, ends up sold at $120 dollars. That web management came out for $5 dollars; He ended up receiving $15 dollars of benefit.

Once the above has happened, it is time to calculate your benefits. The merchant will give you 11% of your capital invested. Now we simplify the return on investment equation, because you decided to leave your capital and even added $5 dollars, having an account with an investment of $105 dollars. Now the utility of your capital will be $11.55 dollars. The equation for the interest or utility generated is as follows:

$$I = Co \times i \times n$$

Where I is the interest generated, Co, the original capital or base or amount invested, i, the interest rate or percentage value that you will receive, and n, the times that the capital moves. So that:

$i = 11 \div 100 = 0.11$

$I = \$105 \times 0.11 \times 1 = \$11.55$

If you realize, before the merchant took the decision to position the product on the web, selling it took a week, now he could sell it the same day he placed it. If you observe, now in a week you have received $ 1.55 dollars over the $10 dollars that you had received a week ago, that is, you are receiving $11.55 in a week, when previously you took 15 days to receive $10 dollars.

On this occasion, the merchant received $3.45 profit. It looks like it has not gone so well, but it was in a week, which is promising. In this opportunity, you do not decide to add to the investment capital, as you did. They are operating with $110 dollars of capital.

The merchant executes the same plan, and in a week returns to have ready the product and to sell it. Applying the same equation of interest, your benefit is again the same, but again weekly. One month has passed and the distribution of benefits is as follows, where you are the investor and the merchant is the entrepreneur, and the value is in dollars.

First 15 days:

Investor: $10
Businessman: $10
Initial capital: $100
Final capital: $110

First 21 days:

Investor: $10 + $11.55 = $21.55
Entrepreneur: $10 + $3.45 = $13.45
Starting capital: $110
Final capital: $110

First 30 days:

Investor: $21.55 + $11.55 = $33.10
Entrepreneur: $13.45 + $3.45 = $16.90
Starting capital: $110
Final capital: $110

The investor is leading the way with the benefits. It seems that the employer is making some mistake in the distribution of the utility. But first we value your decision of positioning on the web; increased from the possible $21.55 that the investor would receive to

$33.10, this being an increase or surplus of $11.55 (53.6% of the expected value). Without adding more capital and without web positioning, I would have received $20 in the month.

The entrepreneur would have earned $20 if he had not positioned the product. He only received $ 16.90, not receiving $ 3.10 dollars.

Let's see possible sources of error. The entrepreneur absorbed the cost of web positioning from his benefit. $10 dollars of the capital lasted 15 days without being touched, and it is likely that this amount will last for months. The businessman had to take from the capital the cost of sale on the web, so that now the cost of production and sale amounted to $105 dollars. Just as he set a profit to the investor, he must have fixed it to himself as well.

Remember that, as an entrepreneur, you must exist and guarantee your quality of life over time. May your desires to grow not take away your life in the attempt? On the other hand, you must make effective use of capital. Those $10 itinerant dollars should have been generating profits.

After observing the behavior of the production and sale of the product, it may be time to encourage and invest or add more money to the base or current capital. However, you should consider a purpose or the employer should set a goal, for example, reduce the time of production of the product by buying a machine that reduces it to at least one unit every two days.

Imagine that you decide to add $15 more to the capital, and the employer, $5. If it is the only thing they have to cover their existential expenses, it may be a lot of investment, taking almost 50% of the profits to reinvest. However, let's see the results. Consider that the machine had a price of $25 dollars. When purchased, the base capital would be $105 dollars of $130 existing. If the production costs remain the same, $105 is sufficient for the business model. Let's see the new behavior of the benefits.

The investor will continue with the same 11% of the profits. The entrepreneur must set his utility also. Imagine that 11% is assigned. Considering this situation and that the product rotate once a month, we would be facing a big failure of return allocation, because we are expecting a 22% return of a product that only generates 14.29%. Before continuing, it is necessary to stop to consider some important aspects in the allocation of sale prices, profit and return of the investment. First, you never drain the capital of production; you cannot make a profit that the product does not leave, because otherwise you would be taking part of the capital. Secondly, any decision you are going to make in financial terms, always considers the worst case.

In the previous situation, the worst case is that the employer sells only one product per month. They would obtain 14.29% and could continue operating, but if they take the 22% expected, they would be draining 7.71% ($8.10), which would be equivalent to having a base capital of $96.90, which would not be enough to continue operating and the business ends unfortunately, the stipulated 11% cannot be assigned. At most 7% each.

If we perform the calculations based on a sale every two days, without injecting more capital, except that the 0.29% surplus of the profits would be added without capitalizing, the following distribution of profits would be obtained.

Ideal Case

With the first sale:

$i = 7 \div 100 = 0.07$
$I = \$105 \times 0.07 \times 1 = \$7.35$
With 15 sales per month:

$I = \$105 \times 0.07 \times 15 = \$110.25$

Each one would be having a return of $110.25 per month. In the worst case, if they only made one sale, each would only see $7.35 per month.

If the machine that managed to speed up production would have cost much or exceeded the effective capacity of those involved, for the worst case, they would already be in trouble. Imagine that this tool had been obtained with a loan of $100 dollars and that they were to pay $10 monthly, they would have had to take their benefits to pay or not pay the loan. Since this was not the case, then they would have had money to pay off the loan.

You have to be careful with the investment, with what you buy, with what you spend ... and do not stop contemplating your benefit in what you do.

For one case and for the other, there is a 0.29% that we have not calculated. This is going to add to the base capital of $105 dollars. To do so, it will be necessary to think about how the way benefits or interests are generated is flowing. For this it will be vital to admit two fundamental concepts of interest or utility.

The case we are dealing with is a conceptual hodgepodge, where on the one hand there is an investment and at the same time we see it produce.

In the financial world there is what is called simple interest and compound interest.

In this particular case, both the investor and the entrepreneur are obtaining their benefits under a simple interest model and the surplus that generates the benefit is not being used to make decisions in the business. That is, both the benefits and the surplus are being evaluated as if it were simple interest. Let's see.

The simple interest is not more than the interests that an initial capital generates in a period of time, which does not accumulate to the capital to produce the interests of the following period. Hence, the above calculations are always being made based on $105 dollars.

Under the simple interest model, the only thing that increases profits is the rotation or sales times of the product, and it does not increase exponentially, but linearly. The greater the rotation, the greater are the benefits. For example, let's look at the behavior.

$I = \$105 \times 0.07 \times 1 = \$7.35$

$I = \$105 \times 0.07 \times 2 = \$14.70$

$I = \$105 \times 0.07 \times 3 = \$22.05$

$\dots$

$I = \$105 \times 0.7 \times 15 = \$110.25$

$I = Co \times i \times n$

As we can see, linearly increases a line in a Cartesian plane. Here, n represents the times that the base capital starts moving.

If we apply the same principle of simple interest, but now to see the initial capital grow, we would have the following:

$$Cf = Co + I$$

Where Cf is the final capital, Co, the initial capital, I, the generated interest. It would have then:

$i = 0.29 \div 100 = 0.0029$

$I = \$105 \times 0.0029 \times 15 = \$4.57$

$Cf = \$105 + \$4.57 = \$109.57$

In 15 simple capitalizations in a month, the initial capital went from $105 to $109.57. This looks good at first glance. It could be a good commercial practice.

Compound interest is the magic formula of wealth. This represents the reason for the suggestion to save and withdraw after a considerable period of time.

We saw that simple interest keeps the same capital invested. If it were a saving under this model, the interest will always be calculated based on the initial capital and it would be as if the interests were on one hand and capital on the other. On the other hand, in compound interest, the interest that is generated at the end of each period is added to the previous capital, so that it serves as a basis for calculating the new interest generated with this new capital.

Compound interest is like a snowball that comes down from a mountain, it grows as it picks up snow particles in its path. Here is the concept:

Compound interest becomes possible when the interest earned each time you capitalize our investment or loan is not withdrawn or paid, but reinvested and added to the initial or principal capital.

The above is the reason why people say "you have to save". It is simply because of the effect over time of compound interest.

The investment you recently made in the employer of the previous case is likely to have been good. Now let's imagine that you invest the same amount in a model that returns compound interest.

The compound interest equations are the following:

$Cf = Co + I$

$I = Co \times i$

$Cf = Co + I$

$Cf = Co + Co \times i$

The common factor here is the Co, then:

$Cf = Co(1 + i)$

But now, when you capitalize, it behaves exponentially, and you have:

$Cf = Co(1 + i)^n$

Before seeing the use of the exponential form, let's see how to get to the last capitalization step by step.

You will invest the $100 dollars at a rate of 7%, they are going to capitalize every two days for a period of 30 days. You will have 15 capitalizations during the 30 days, just like your previous experience. In the following equation, p is the calculated period, C capital of such period.

$Cf = Co(1 + i)$

$C1 = \$100.00(1 + 0.07) = \$107.00$
$C2 = \$107.00(1 + 0.07) = \$114.49$
$C3 = \$114.49(1 + 0.07) = \$122.50$
$C4 = \$122.50(1 + 0.07) = \$131.08$
$C5 = \$131.08(1 + 0.07) = \$140.26$
$C6 = \$140.26(1 + 0.07) = \$150.07$

$C7 = \$150.07(1 + 0.07) = \$160.58$
$C8 = \$160.58(1 + 0.07) = \$171.82$
$C9 = \$171.82(1 + 0.07) = \$183.85$
$C10 = \$183.85(1 + 0.07) = \$196.72$
$C11 = \$196.72(1 + 0.07) = \$210.49$
$C12 = \$210.49(1 + 0.07) = \$225.22$
$C13 = \$225.22(1 + 0.07) = \$240.98$
$C14 = \$240.98(1 + 0.07) = \$257.85$
$C15 = \$257.85(1 + 0.07) = \$275.90$

In the previous process, we see how our capital grows in each capitalization period. I wanted to follow that form, so that you could grasp the power of saving or the reason why people save.

While simple interest grows linearly, here it does so exponentially. This is the secret.

For the equation with exponential component, we would have the following in capitalization number 15:

$Cf = \$100(1 + 0.07)^{15}$

$C15 = \$275.90$

The advantage of this equation is that you can determine how much your capital will end up in any capitalization period, using the initial amount only, so that, for example, in period 7:

$Cf = \$100(1 + 0.07)^7$

$C7 = \$260.58$

This is what would happen if you withdrew your savings or investment in period 7; you would receive $260.58, for a generated interest of $160.58 dollars.

The interest or profit generated in the 15 capitalizations could be calculated as follows:

$I = Cf - Co$

$I = C15 - Co$

$I = \$275.90 - \$100.00$

$I = \$175.90$

The key to the generation of wealth is in the reinvestment, using the generated interest to continue generating more interests.

Under this model, compared to the simple interest, you have achieved greater utility. In the first one, you generated $110.25 of profit without increasing the investment capital; you simply reinvested the same capital in each capitalization ($105.00). In the second, you approach to double the profit, generating $175.90 dollars of return in 15 capitalizations, leaving the interest to be added to your base or initial capital ($100.00).

What you just captured, is an ideal case, however, it would be a reality if they offered you such ease in real life.

If you went to a bank with the intention of saving, you will see that each institution will have its investment options. For personal accounts, they are likely to offer you an annual interest rate with annual capitalization.

When we refer to a saving or investment capitalized at a certain time, we mean that it is the time when interest is added to the initial or previous capital, in the case of compound interest.

Within the time capitalization hear often invest or save t n number of years with capitalizations per year, at a rate of interest i whenever capitalizes investment, which is what we've been trying so far.

The most common capitalizations in the market could be the following: annual, semi-annual, quarterly,

quarterly, bimonthly, monthly, even fortnightly, weekly, daily capitalization...

We must pay attention to the times that capitalize our money in a certain time, because the number of capitalizations depends on our profit or utility, in addition to the interest rate. I reinforce this idea by the simple mathematical relation of direct proportionality. The higher n in a stipulated time at a constant rate i, the higher return on investment. For example, you decide to invest $100 in a B bank, for a year at a 10% semi-annual interest rate, and $100 in another bank O, for a year at a 10% quarterly rate. Which will be more convenient if both use compound interest?

Data:

Co = $100

i = 10%

t = 1 year

n =?

Solution:

Bank B

n = 2, because one year has two semesters.

$Cf = \$100(1 + 0.10)^2$

$Cf = \$121.00$

For an interest I of $21.00 in one year.

Bank O

n = 4, because one year has four quarters.

$Cf = \$100(1 + 0.10)^4$

$Cf = \$146.41$

For an interest I of $46.41 in one year.

Remember that this is an ideal case. Most likely, whoever offers the highest number of capitalizations will give you a lower interest rate, but you should still calculate to compare and determine which bank gives you the most value.

The advantage of having several capitalizations for a certain time is that if you decide to withdraw your capital, you will probably leave with a few capitalizations in your favor. Imagine that you deposit the same $100 at a rate of 10%, but capitalized annually and withdraw it before the year. You will have gone with the same $ 100 dollars, for not waiting for the year and its capitalization. In contrast, in the previous cases, if you take your savings after six months, at least you will have taken the interest of the first capitalization of bank B ($10 dollars), and the interest of two capitalizations of bank O, $21 dollars.

After having traveled this road through the world of interests, investments and savings, it is worth noting once again that material wealth is achieved with discipline and patience, in addition to the other ingredients. Whoever withdraws from the investment before, declares his possible exit from the path of the rich.

The key to economic wealth and financial independence lies in the feedback of capital. This declares the compound interest equation.

$$Cf = Co(1 + i)^n$$

And we see that riches accumulate exponentially.

If you do not pursue wealth through savings and prefer investment in projects with a higher return than a bank could give you, simply do not lose sight of the risks that each path offers you. You will have the necessary skill to face whichever you choose.

In case you venture to follow the steps of the big investment, here are some of the risks you should consider when investing, according to the author and researcher David Bendel Hertz in his treatise "Risk Analysis in Capital Investment", Harvard Business Review (September-October 1979), pp. 169-181:

1. Market size

2. Sale prices

3. Market growth rate

4. Market share

5. Useful life (time horizon)

6. Total investment

7. Residual value

8. Operating costs

9. Fixed costs

10. Investment cost

11. Unit variable cost

12. Expected value in physical units of the product

Other authors divide the risk into economic risk and financial risk.

Economic risk refers to the nature or type of company and market where it operates. Hence, you have to take these factors into account in order not to end up losing your capital in a risky investment.

When investing in a company, you must know what it sells, its demand and how its sale is affected as the economy fluctuates.

Suppose the case that your target company markets a product that can be sold by any other company, then the competitiveness and barriers for anyone wishing to enter that market, do not exist. So it is not a feasible option at first sight. It is good to choose companies whose products differ from the market in order to have a lower investment risk. Of the demand is not said, the product must be demandable and endure the difficult times, that is, sell almost always or always.

It is necessary to know if the costs may vary over time, so that the production can adjust to the demand and achieve the desired utility. When the costs remain fixed regardless of the demand, it makes the investment very risky.

Imagine that the company where you have decided to invest has fixed costs of $10,000.00 dollars per month and sales have fallen, because a competitor entered the market. Initially, the company would receive about $5,000.00 monthly return. Suppose that now you have to direct 50% of the profits to cover the costs, you just stopped receiving $2,500.00 dollars in that month, because right now you could not vary your costs. This behavior is common when a company depends on a specific number of people to operate; Even if production goes down, you cannot fire your staff or perhaps break agreements in haste. This is the meaning of the cost structure.

Now we will have the difficulty of the one who wants to grow. If you want to invest and have low risk, you will have to consider the number of customers and suppliers of the target company.

A company with few customers and a range or limited offer or, well, a single supplier is the one that provides all the products, constitutes a risky investment, because right now it does not satisfy the demand or it is without a supplier and the business falls. If the opposite occurs, it has many customers and many suppliers that offer variety in both quality and types of products, and then this is an investment to be considered.

It happens that the company is perhaps complying with the previous conditions, however, it does not have a feasible line of distribution and sale of the products, or else it is very difficult for the product to reach the final consumer. We are facing a problem that hinders the sale due to difficulty of the distribution of the product or its cost of marketing. This would be a risky investment, although perhaps your investment is necessary to improve the channels of distribution and marketing of the products.

It could happen that your target company exceeds previous expectations, however, the sale prices are changing, customers receive credits for too long, accounts receivable are that they do not support more debts, suppliers give you very little time to pay the raw material ... the fact is that this projects a lot of instability, so that commercial conditions are difficult. With a scenario like this, do not even think about it, unless you want to save the company and reinvent the rules and that they are offering you a high rate of return, which is even questionable before this description of the case.

On the other hand, continuing with the types of risk, we have the financial risk. It is necessary to know how the company supports its investments and how many resources are foreign, what are the costs of use and term in which they will be returned.

Imagine that you decide to invest, but the company operates with financed and long-term capital, in addition to using rented machinery to create their products, they would be variables that could involve some risk. Now, if your financing is short-term, it could be considered, or it may be long-term and there will be little time to pay.

If the indebtedness of the company is sustainable or of quality, there should be no doubt. It could be feasible to invest.

You have to be careful with investing in indebted companies.

Many lines back, it was said that to be rich you learn, that you have to educate yourself, that you have to be cautious, calculating, wait for the right moment, have patience and hunter strategies, be a domesticated wolf, pay attention to details, among other qualities necessary to be rich.

So far some touches of the equation of wealth and the risks behind such a simple equation when you decide to use it to invest in companies where everything is possible.

Having known some of the risks to be contemplated before and during an investment, you can forge an idea of why few can be called or become rich. However, knowledge makes you free, opening you to new horizons and giving you the opportunity to become what you want.

The formula of wealth should be taught from childhood, in order to increase the likelihood that new rich people will be able to emerge. In some financial institutions, child savings is promoted, which is good. But the same should be taught and cultivate the culture of the rich in childhood, in terms of attitudes and values aimed at wealth.

The awakening of greatness

Curiosity killed the cat.
But he still has six lives left.

We live under an illusion, under the belief that, practically, everything is done or resolved and we sleep on the laurels of the believed glory.

Passivity kills the creativity and curiosity of many who today want to be rich. Some crave it, others were born in the cradles of wealth, but both the one and the other are suffering from the effect everything is done or we are not going to reinvent the wheel. The truth is that many things are done, but if they were not improved every day, it would be time they had disappeared from the market. We have always been reinventing.

If everything is done, why have not we reached Mars? If everything is done, why have we not been able to overcome the depths of the oceans? If not everything is done, why is there no system that is infallible? If everything is done, why are there diseases that sadly end with humanity? If everything is done, why is there hunger in the world? If everything is done, why do men kill each other? If everything is done, why is there so much lack in humanity?

Not everything is done. Something is done. And if you want to be rich, you'll have to start exploring new opportunities and discover what needs to be improved in the world.

We must begin to awaken curiosity, to explore, to look for details in things, to erase popular expressions of conformism. There is still a lot to do.

The illusion that has created the technological advance that everything seems to be done is only a marketing projection. The entrepreneurs and influents that we see in social networks, youtube, instagram, facebook, can be counted with respect to the world population. It needs more people integrated to the generation of solutions to current problems.

Global warming is still there, the melting of glaciers at the poles is an obvious fact. Could you say that this problem is solved? If you want to be rich, there are many opportunities available. It is up to you to take the step or not.

It is common to say that simple inventions are already made, that, therefore, it is difficult to find an invention that will catapult you towards the economic peak. It is likely that by increasing our level of introspection, we can find solutions to the complex problems that we are experiencing today.

Solving complex problems is as easy as dividing and winning. Divide and conquer is a type of algorithm to solve complex operations in programming languages. It is the technique of abstracting a problem and solving it by its parts. The detail is that we tend to see the whole problem, fed by the perception of others and we end up putting it bigger than necessary.

Divide and conquer is a collaborative strategy to solve complex situations. For example, we have the problem of access to fresh or drinking water and daily we waste hundreds of gallons while we carry out our daily activities. Solution: Let's all collaborate, using less, closing the tap, destroying nature less. Every time someone turns off the tap while brushing, he is already contributing to the solution.

It is likely that if I remember the tap, it is because someone has unleashed a viral message about what our inappropriate use of the water resource represents. It has already begun to contribute to the solution. Strategy: a striking message with verifiable information. Content: collaboration of all to reduce the amount of water we waste every day.

To awaken greatness is to awaken sensitivity and begin to respond with innovative solutions to the situations that arise every day. For those who believe in chance, wealth could visit you doing the right thing, what you love.

Success programming

Success is an undomesticated animal.
It's yours when you domesticate it.

At the beginning of the treaty, it was said that to be successful you learn, just as you could learn to be happy. It was also stated that there was a difference between being successful and feeling successful.

Educate the brain so that you always see success, is educate it so that you always see the opportunity in everything you undertake. It is preparing you to grow through any experience. It is to plant the seed of optimism, so that it germinates, grows and projects good attitude towards any eventuality.

Being successful and feeling successful are different, but they complement each other. Having reached a goal, however minimal, we should have the feeling of success. As I enjoy small successes and enjoy them, I project to the brain that what I am consuming or experiencing is good. This is how this then begins to feel comfort, to release the neurotransmitters that keep me happy and energetic to continue advancing to the next goal. Hence, being successful feeds on positive sensations; when this does not happen, even if you are succeeding, you cannot appreciate it and the probability that you end up frustrated is high.

Rationalize situations a little and tell the brain or convince yourself that what is happening is good, helps build a positive life and leads to the next success. We must make each experience a success.

If you do not feel it, others will not feel it either. They will see in you a person with a dull face, perhaps bitter and will not value what you have just achieved.

All this to take the good side of situations, is summarized in being grateful, in appreciating the opportunity you had to improve. A successful person is grateful and this projects a leadership ingredient, because others appreciate such an attitude.

Success arises from the cultivation of calm, reflection and constructive action. In the face of the imminent danger of a situation, the common thing is to see and catalog it at first sight as harmful, and possibly run away.

Imagine waiting for an executive summary of an employee. The standard is to be delivered on a page, with graphics and conclusions. It happens that he has given you three pages during the stipulated meeting before the other members of the top management. You may decide to get angry, because the summary does not meet the requirements. However, you stop, look at the document and notice that the extra pages represent the details of the sales failure points of the month, so you can justify to everyone that the sales fell because the sellers were visiting the business during lunch hours or at inappropriate times.

Keep calm, reflect and then act. You cannot see the opportunities while you are angry. And do not forget to be grateful. It was not what you expected, but he did you a favor.

You have to educate the brain to see the good in what you do. If you have eaten hot pepper or chili, you may have noticed that the sensation is strong, but in a short time the brain gets used to it and returns a feeling of pleasure or adrenaline. It releases what you just expect in the face of pain, endorphins and dopamine.

Imagine you are going to a vet to buy a dog. While you pass in front of the cages, you see how loud the dogs bark at you and you even get scared, but you keep moving forward in the search. When you reach the end of the corridor, you are stunned by the loud bark and blow that the last canine gives to its cage. The scare is great; you are marked by the impact and you go to the administrator.

You tell the owner or manager that they should not have such a dog for sale as a pet. He responds with a smile and expresses that some people like that race and that because they are so powerful, they place him at the end of the corridor. You stay thoughtful about his response. After a few minutes thinking, you decide to buy it. They have a hard time riding it to the truck with everything and cage. While driving to the house, it makes thunderous movements, which even vibrate the vehicle.

When you get to the house, you prepare to download it. The dog hits the cage and shows its teeth, wanting to fall on you. You place it in the place determined for it and take a break.

Later, you address the dog. It's just as rabid. You stop, you look into his eyes and you notice how he calms down and even starts to move his tail. You just conquered your defender.

This is how success is programmed. It does not arrive, it is there. You just have to stay calm, stop to find out, and if it looks dangerous, proceed to tame it.

Precious stones are stones until an artist decides to carve them and turn them into jewels. Success is created.

To program success is to program your mind to see opportunities in everything that happens to you.

The wealth programming

No one decides to be born rich or poor.
You decide for the next one.

Wealth has patterns as well as the musical notes of a song.

If you remember the farmer, you will remember that the pigs grow as you feed them over time. If you remember the compound interest equation, you will realize that the final capital grows to the extent that you allow the interest earned to be added to the initial or previous capital; the benefits added to the previous amount, generate new benefits.

If you look, there is a pattern. If you stay on the curve, you keep growing. It is a matter of repeating the act and opening the mind and heart towards what is to come.

We are born without deciding, but we live by decision. We do not decide in which family nucleus to be born, but what will be the nucleus for the next offspring.

If we were not born in a golden cradle, then it is time to start building the cradle of our next generation. It's a matter of knowing the options and how they work.

Option 1: The savings classic

For passive minds, not very daring, saving is the sure way to generate wealth. Be aware of the time factor to see the benefits grow.

If saving is your decision, look for the financial institution that offers the best rate of interest and the one that capitalizes more per year.

Remember that you save what you have. After having calculated all your expenses, part of the surplus is what you will choose to save. Under this model, you may not get there so fast if your mission is to become rich.

Through the savings option, your riches will be greater depending on the initial amount you deposit. This could depend on your income and your expenses.

When we are really determined to one day have a capital that allows us to make decisions towards new horizons, such as starting our own business, going on vacation or perhaps complementing our pension funds, then we tend to cut expenses, to live a more controlled life; we learn to prioritize, to buy what we really need, without necessarily draining our quality of life, because many of the things we have, in general, do not need them, we have simply created needs or created them for us. When we begin to put this behavior into practice, then we begin to become the rich we want to be.

Returning to savings, imagine that after having calculated all our expenses, of our income we are $200 dollars monthly. Each month we will take them and add them to the savings account. We will assume that we will follow that practice for a period of 5 to 10 years. We will look for the market rate that returns us the most profit, which will depend on the times capitalized per year and the interest rate itself. Commercial banks will offer us compound interest; therefore, we will proceed to use the compound interest equation.

Let's imagine the average case of the banking offer of the market: 8% annual, capitalization semiannually, that is, 4% per period, because the year has two semesters. The equation to convert the rate to the value per period is:

$$i = \frac{Annual\ interest\ rate}{conversion\ frequency}$$

In this case, the conversion frequency is 2, because the year has two semesters. Remember that "i" is the interest rate that we will use for our calculations.

$$i = \frac{0.08}{2} = 0.04$$

Now let's proceed with the compound interest equation.

$$Cf = Co(1 + i)^n$$

Let's imagine that we make our first deposit of $200 on January 1. On June 30 we will have our first capitalization. On December 31 we will have the next one.

As of June 30:

$$Cf = \$200.00(1 + 0.04)^1$$

$$Cf = \$208.00$$

At December 31:

$$Cf = \$208.00(1 + 0.04)^1$$

$$Cf = \$216.32$$

To the full year:

$$Cf = \$200.00(1 + 0.04)^2$$

$$Cf = \$216.32$$

Remember that n is the number of capitalization periods in a given time and that the rate i to use is the one with which you will capitalize in each period.

In 5 years, we will have 10 capitalizations. That is to say:

$$n = conversion\ frequency \times time$$

$$n = 2 \times 5 = 10$$

Our capital in 5 years, considering only the single deposit of $ 200 dollars, will be:

$$Cf = \$200.00(1 + 0.04)^{10}$$

$Cf = \$296.05$

In 10 years:

$Cf = \$200.00(1 + 0.04)^{20}$

$Cf = \$438.22$

If we cancel the account at 10 years, we will have earned $238.22 dollars.

What you just saw, is only for a single deposit, if you keep saving $200 in $200 each month, the story will be different.

Consider that we will save the same amount, but annually, that is, each year we will take $200 dollars and we will take them to the account. On this occasion, we will be keeping records in the deposits, in 10 years we will have made 10 deposits.

To be able to make the calculations of the final capital of the previous case, we will have to use a system, because it could become tedious to do it manually.

Rethinking the initial case, we have 4% semiannual, initial capital of $200 dollars, adding $200 annually, after finishing each period a year, for a period of 10 years. Under these conditions, we will have accumulated $2,726.93 dollars. In those ten years, you have deposited $2,000.00 dollars; you have generated a profit or utility of $726.93 dollars. This was only with annual deposits of $200 dollars; if we did it monthly, another was the benefit story.

You may understand that right now these benefits are not enough to get rich. If in your best case you can save $2,400.00 annually, which would be about $200.00 per month, you will end up having $32,723.12 in ten years, for a profit of $8,723.12 (this taking the same initial data of the investment, increasing the amount of the deposits). The truth is that if your income does not allow it, you will be forced to reach wealth.

If you are worried about this option, it may be necessary to remember that it is not becoming a millionaire, it is to adopt the culture of the rich, and this is one of them.

There is a feeling called security. When you save, you are forging security in your life, and at the same time, that security offers you other opportunities that result in tranquility and such tranquility transforms into increased probability of success and happiness. A person, who feels calm about their future, has a more open mind to see opportunities that a stressed person cannot see. Here is part of the secret of saving.

When you save, you can put your mind to fly, establish plans that will keep you motivated in the decision and that motivation will make you more productive. Taking the first step is the key.

Imagine that you have been saving $2,400.00 dollars per year while working in a bakery. Your plan is to start your own company in the ten years of the case referred to above. In that time, you have been learning to develop your own strategies to attract and improve sales. You have become an expert in cake making. Once the saving period has elapsed, you will be able to make the decision of your dream. You may have to finance something, but at least you have an amount that will help you take the first step.

You have to be careful with sensationalist ideas. Remember that the rich must be realistic in what they do. The idea is not to take out the lottery, but to build a solid base of assets, which allows you to stay in time and enjoy a certain quality of life. Feel the precedent.

Most television shows sell the extraordinary and, in the process, anyone with low self-esteem could end up believing that it will only come to something in life if it is extraordinary, a genius, a celebrity. The truth is that celebrities and geniuses are numbered. The population average is normal and from that normality it is that everyone who wants to be great must be born.

Contrary to the above, believing that you will only succeed if you are a genius or a celebrity, you should refute that it is a belief, not necessarily a reality. You just believe it and it is a possible false belief; It does not mean that it will be like that. Now, you have to be careful with beliefs, and especially with those that attempt against your dreams. We can all be what we want to be and make what we dream come true.

Going back to saving, it is important that you know that just as you will have a few extra dollars in ten years or in the time you decide, there is also an economic phenomenon called inflation, increase in the prices of the products, which could translate into a low performance of what you end up receiving.

The above is just a factor. The reservation is made so that right now you are not going to believe that a dream is being sold to you. It is good to be rich, but a rich aware of the whole.

The rich have to be aware of the variables that affect their decisions. If you do not take them into account, you could end up failing in your attempts.

This has been the way of saving. It is maybe not the best, but good to grow it. When you save, you are giving the bank your money to administer it, generate utility and return part of it. As such, you do not have to worry about how it makes you generate interest, but I do tell you that the reason why you do not receive such high rates of return, is because banks have a structure of employees who are responsible for getting your money to hands that put it to produce in business in exchange for a certain interest.

When a bank returns an 8% annual interest for your money saved, it is because right now it has invested or borrowed at a rate so convenient that it allows it to exist as a bank, maintain its employ and that it is somewhat profitable for the client that receives the money. It is a mere exchange and representation of your money.

By taking your money to a financial institution, you are depositing your trust to generate utility with it. Likewise, you are downloading from a possible responsibility to lend it yourself to a third party and assume the stress of being charged and the risk of not being paid.

If you see the market rate low for your money, you may already understand it better. You are buying tranquility, and as you see, it has a price.

When we understand the financial dynamics, we begin to stop suffering, because we diminish our ignorance. We no longer have to say that banks are thieves. We learn that they are businesses and that we all want to win.

Saving is your decision.

Option 2: The attraction of investment

The investment is somewhat similar to saving; although the saving is to invest, but through a third party. When you decide to invest, the first image that comes to mind is that of a project that requires capital and you have the possibility to inject it.

Many people are willing to invest in promising projects, but at the same time they are afraid of economic and financial risks; they are concerned about the profitability and the risk of the investment. To avoid this world of uncertainty, what remains for the investor is to know the risks involved in a given investment, in order to know if it is feasible or not.

While dealing with risk approaches due to the types of economic risks and financial risks, some investment analyzes were made in a rough way, trying to forge an idea of how to decide on one variable or another. Now we will proceed to make another approach for a possible investment, but contemplating variables of the Hertz treaty.

Imagine that we will invest in a rice factory, but that this factory is the United States of America.

First let's consider the market analysis. To this we will assign four variables:

Size of the market

It refers to the quantity of products in units that the target market can consume.

According to the FAO (United Nations Organization for Food and Agriculture), 759.6 million tons of rice (503.9 million tons of processed rice) were harvested in the world by 2017 (Rice Market Monitoring, April 2018). Assuming that the processed rice will be the amount consumed by the market, and then the size of our world market is 503.9 million tons. It happens that the United States of America only produces 2% (FAO, 2006) of rice in the world. If we are only going to market in this country, then we must define our market, which would go from 503.9 to 10.1 million tons of processed rice and 15.2 million tons in shell.

Sale prices

It deals with the prices at which the products or services will be sold, contemplating the profit margins.

By March 2019, paddy rice was selling at $238 a tonne in Chicago (https://arroz.com/tags/estados-unidos, March 14, 2019).

Market growth rate

It is about the percentage speed with which the market grows, according to predictions based on the consumption history of previous periods.

From 2016 to 2017, production increased by 0.6% or 4.5 million tons. For this period, the market growth rate was 0.6%.

Market share

It refers to the percentage of the market that can be covered by the company if it decides to offer its products or services.

The participation of the United States of America in the world rice market is 2% (FAO, 2006).

Now let's record the investment cost analysis. To this we will assign three variables:

Total inversion

It is the total cost involved from setting up the company, putting it to produce and getting the product or service to the customer.

As an example, and to get closer to reality, we will add 30% to the fixed costs to have our total investment. So this will be $ 2,307.2 million dollars.

Lifespan (time horizon)

It refers to the value that would be recovered in machinery and real estate if it were desired to sell them at the end of their useful life. It is about the depreciation they suffer over time. To determine it, the depreciation method is used according to the existing tax equity law.

The useful time of rice machinery is around 10 years.

Residual value

It is the value with which the buildings, constructions, work vehicles, machinery and equipment, telephone exchanges, mobile machines and office installation, among others, would end after applying the percentage of depreciation in the useful life.

Suppose that the depreciation of the machinery used for production, will end at 10% in 10 years for the investment made. As an example, we will apply 10% to the fixed costs. Then we will have a remnant of $177.5 million dollars.

Other costs would be the following:

Operating costs

They are the costs of keeping the company in operation. In this group are the operating costs, unit variable cost, cost of the investment, among others.

Between 1991 and 2011, to produce 1 ton of rice, you had to invest $114.5 dollars. That is, $114.5 / ton.

Fixed costs

It refers to costs that do not change even if production changes. Here appear the expenses of administrative personnel, rent, among others.

Between 1991 and 2011, to produce 1 ton of rice, you had to invest $114.5 dollars. If our market is 15.2

million tons, then we will have a total investment of $1,774.75 million dollars.

Expected value in physical units of the product

It is the amount that is expected to be produced by space and available resources. It refers to the production capacity.

Between 1991 and 2011, the average yield in a year of production was 7.1t / ha (tons per hectare).

If we wanted to calculate the return on investment based on the data we have, we would have:

For 2009, 1 acre (0.40ha) of rice left a profit of $ 229 dollars ($572.5 per hectare). Assuming that by 2019 it would remain constant (10 years later), planting the 1.2 million hectares destined for rice production, there would be a return of approximately $687 million dollars per year.

$$ROE = \frac{\$687.0}{\$2,307.2} = 0.2978$$

This means a return of 29.78% per year.

In order to complete this analysis, we would also have to add economic and financial risks. For example, the degree of import penetration of US rice for 1990-2010 was 6%, practically satisfying domestic demand; however, it is known that for this period, its indicator of tradability was 41.6%, representing this an excess of supply of rice, meaning that the business model of this product is oriented for export, having then the competitiveness factor against the world. This country is in the fourth place as a world exporter, being above India, Vietnam, and Thailand, which occupies the first place.

All the previous approaches are based on existing data. The alterations made in some cases, are intended to exemplify. It is an empirical process, based on raw data. When making a serious investment, it is necessary to contemplate more variables and simulate each one in probabilistic models. Risk Analysis in Capital Investment by David B. Hertz could be useful or advisory.

Make this tour of important investment concepts, so that there is awareness when making decisions in whatever the market.

In his book, The Fear of Freedom, Erich Fromm states that capitalism freed the individual, became the master of his destiny, where he is the risk, his the benefit. To eliminate the fears in the investment, we must know, and it is the path that has been traveled so far.

Knowing leads the individual to decrease the error rate and increase their probability of success. Freedom is conquered with knowledge.

If you are going to invest, start with scale projects, and as you acquire skills and confidence, then you increase the bet. This will lower the levels of uncertainty and risks. Ideally, you would specialize in the market with two or three products.

Option 3: The dream of your own business

Having gone through the path of the saver, where all the risks are assumed by the financial institution; the decision of the investment, in which both the investor and the entrepreneur assume the risks; Now we have arrived at the moment in which you decide to assume everything, be an investor and an entrepreneur, where yours is the risk and yours is the benefit.

As has been your decision, now let's start with brief strokes to proceed to start your own business.

Remember that the mission is to be rich, in the short and long term.

Wanting to have a company is like wanting to have a child, like wanting to have a car, among other desires that involve great responsibility. When you want something, the first quality that should ignite in the mind of the rich, is planning. The rich is planned, just as wealth is planned, because in itself, it is nourished by many attitudes and aptitudes, as has been stated throughout this treaty. Planning for everything is the requirement.

If you want to have a child, probably, the stable sequence to follow in time is to find and establish a relationship of courtship, determine if the couple would like to marry and have children in the future, ask for marriage and see if they accept, marry, establish a plan between them, decide how long they could be prepared to bring the first offspring to the world, get pregnant, take care of themselves and feed themselves well during pregnancy, wait six or nine months, go to the birth, give a successful welcome to life outside the womb and there begins the new history and the new challenges. It is possible that something was missing.

The above is the same as what will happen to your business intention.

Below is a list of requirements or steps to reach the point of concretization of your business dream.

ONE. Want to have the company, know what your passion is and will be in life, that you will be identified with the lifestyle.

TWO. Define the business line you want to follow, define your market.

THREE. Be clear on how you will finance the business, whether with your own capital, borrowed or mixed. The chosen type will reveal multiple situations to be considered. If there were to be financing, consider the following:

A. Verify your credit history. This could be a determining factor when acquiring financing.
B. Request an estimate of your payment capacity and indebtedness. The financial institution could give you your current score or financial positioning, which is a reference to be able to receive loans.
C. Propose to the financial institution how much you will need to start your business. There they will estimate you the maximum they could lend you, the lowest possible interest rate and the maximum time to pay. Each variable and its value will depend on the type of loan you wish to acquire.

It is important to recognize that the bank will be acting as an investor. Consequently, it will evaluate the credit risk that you represent for it. It is the probability that you do not have enough funds to comply with the agreement, for example, that your income is now lower than expected, that the company fails, or that if it were an employee, he loses his job.

If you take a loan while employed, it will be a personal loan. In general, this type of financing has one of the highest interest rates in the market, because the risk is higher. It's about unsecured loans; the only support is that you are employed.

Financing is also available with guarantors or co-signers. These could be easier to acquire if you have a solvent guarantor. Their rates tend to be more comfortable. They could have better payment facilities.

Another possible option is that you take the loan as a company, which will imply that you are already operating and that it transmits confidence for the investment based on evidence of economic movement. These financings tend to be more comfortable in the sense of interest rate, balance time ... because they tend to have a lower risk if the company is promising.

Depending on the jurisdiction, there may be banks with projects or lines of business aimed at financing entrepreneurs or small entrepreneurs. This would be a facility in your favor.

Imagine that you have received the loan at a fixed rate, which is supposed to stay that way for a certain time, after that time has passed, the increase will depend on the phenomenon of inflation, which constitutes one of the financial risks. That is why financing does not tolerate fixed rates for a long time, because it depends on the economic' stability of the jurisdiction. It could happen that at the time of taking the loan the inflation was at 5% and, after a time, it will shoot up at 10% or more. The bank will make the adjustments to continue compensating.

D. Evaluate if you will need a partner to carry out your business. So that it can help you with financing and legal considerations.

FOUR. Choose the product in which you will specialize. For starting, at least two or three key products if your mission is to cover a certain variety of the market. Everything will depend on what you really want to offer.

FIVE. Do a market study, to know if what you really want to offer is what the market really wants, just to know the disposition, experience and real needs of the consumer.

SIX. Create a work plan, establish time and stages to be exhausted. Study more background market behavior, compare the movement of the product in other markets.

SEVEN. Make a list of possible suppliers for your product range. Classify them between those that offer credit and those that do not. Consider the delivery times of the products or raw material.

EIGHT. Prepare your document or business proposal, considering as many variables as possible. Apply the analysis of economic and financial risks. In this stage, all the steps to open the company are exhausted. Here are the sub-stages of this step:

A. Define the name of your business. It is always difficult to find a business name that can be identified with what is pursued, since it is creative, memorable, easy to write, that does not generate confusion, among other details, that does not exist in the local market.
B. Design your logo. This will be the image or graphic idea with which you will accompany your commercial name. Same as the previous case, it is expected to be creative, memorable, and possibly represent your business idea.

C. Submit the previous steps before the institutions of registration of names and trademarks.
D. Make the commercial register. This will give you legal authority to operate in the market and recognition and trust by the client.
E. Perform other procedures that are necessary in your jurisdiction.

NINE. Prior to having all the operating conditions: legal person, employee, products, etc., start the company. Here you will show that you have the attitudes and skills to succeed in your business.

Option 4: The work combination

There are people who complement working hours as employees with extra ticket activities. They are dedicated to the sale of products by catalog in free time, they explore new opportunities.

With regard to the above, to the extra activity for extra tickets, the important thing would be to put the same criteria, as if it were a company, so that it does not lose character and motivation is gone. That is, it is not a decision because right now the person is desperate to complete income to meet their expenses; it should be another life project.

Each step addressed must be serious. If you do not put this ingredient, the target market will not have confidence in what is done or, well, take the first product on credit, for example, and end up not paying, because right now there is no structure to carry payment records, tracking debts, or, well, because the product was taken by a friend and you are afraid to charge him.

Every time it is sold, you cannot forget that it is a company and that you yourself are the first company.

There are expenses, there are risks, you have to contemplate profit and that capital is maintained and grows over time.

This option adds stress and removes opportunity and style to the concept of rich. However, without forgetting that saving should be in all options, discipline and work is the path to wealth.

Option 5: Manage existing riches

If the family you come from got wealth and business, you could prepare to be part of the business, manage...

For this purpose, strengthening financial education and business administration are pertinent ways.

Follow the steps of the rich, is prudence.

Being Rich –for short and long term-

Feel it, imagine it, and believe it.
Make it a lifestyle.

There is a point at which to believe so much and deeply in something; we end up becoming that something, even without reaching it. Because believing in it transforms you.

Being rich is like making a recipe and fulfilling it step by step, so that we stay as specified.

In the short term, the mission is to allow oneself to be transformed by that which leads to desire. Repeating and changing over time are the two elements that will guarantee the realization of all dreams in the long term.

It is necessary to adopt the ways of thinking of the rich, all the attitudes that define it. On the path of wealth, we find many qualities that characterize it.

In the short term, do not spend today what you may need tomorrow. Be measured in expenses. Do not exceed the income wanting to indulge all tastes. You have to manage as if you were a company.

In the short term, avoid lustful proposals. Be careful with the advantages offered by credit cards. Your money is borrowed; it is not ours, and what we spend must be possible to pay with our income. In case of using them, only for emergencies; Going partying, shopping or tasting delicacies with this resource are not emergencies.

In short term, everything in its time, the patience to wait for the right moment. You have to fine-tune the tastes; only what is necessary and pleasant to move forward. Do not despair, because if you acquire something without really being able, your next income could end up committed to pay debts for compulsive acquisition. It is a requirement to control oneself, to work on emotions.

In the short term, do not please when you really cannot. Do not feign, the simpler, the better. The rich man is simple and delicate in his tastes. He pleases people only when it is necessary and convenient.

If in case you surround yourself with wealthy people and you still do not have the facility to compete in your social circle, do what you can, but do not worry about matching yourself. Keep the simplicity and good taste, but do not want to give your tastes. The rich will appreciate more your humility and good attitudes that pretend to pretend what you have not yet reached, especially that of having money to spend.

Where there is wealth, it exists because you take care of what you have. We have already said, the rich measure what he spends, and spend as long as he understands that it is convenient and have the previous entry to support the expense.

The rich can practice kindness, but goodness with measure, because if today you get rid of your production capital to help, it is likely that tomorrow you will have to close your company.

The idea is not to restrict oneself to the extreme. It is to be rational in each given step. If you take care of every decision, you will be taking care of your physical and mental health.

In the short term, it seeks to maintain physical and mental health. The body does not need the exquisite dishes of expensive restaurants to live. You can take a healthy diet with food from home, know what you are really eating, to know what will happen to your health in the short and long term.

Mental health depends on the lifestyle you lead. If you go to a restaurant and spend the meal money of the month on two courses, it is likely that both your physical and mental health will be compromised. It is a perspective failure that ends in stress and anxiety, and a physical performance that may be drained.

You have to take care of even the energy that is transformed, and I do not say spend, because a return must bring such an investment.

When we begin to use the word investment, we will begin to improve our lives and become true rich. The rich always invests, in the broad sense of the word.

If you cultivate people who add you, you are investing. Surround yourself with people that complement you, that contribute to your walk. Even just have a good vibes, that is positive, that spreads joy and happiness.

Make sure that what comes out of you, in thought, word and deed, returns with the result of compound interest.

Think of the return of any investment. If you go to the movies once a week or a month, which return to you stress release, reactivate your energies to be more productive in the work week. If you talk to someone, let the content of the conversation edify you, whether you listen to them to learn, or if you listen to them to help them.

When you give, you receive. And you will always receive as much as you give, such as savings and compound interest. But remember not to exceed your possibilities. When you help someone, you are really helping yourself. When you get rid of your time and / or your assets, you do not become less rich, because the equation of interest will return alone. You invest, you receive exponentially.

In the short term, keep your relationships active. It is like keeping you saving in a constant or disciplined way. You do not know when you will have to go to your savings. You do not know at what moment these relationships return your accumulated interest.

Never end a relationship, unless there are dangers and you have to separate the waters, to know who you are with. Simply, establish distance, the time also returns your interest, healing wounds and making you stronger. Leave open relationships to new possibilities.

In the short term, avoid suffering for the inevitable and become aware of reality. Being realistic does not rule out the need to increase our ability to recover from falls, resilience. The rich must move forward despite adversity. Difficulties make you stronger or catapult you further.

In the long term, it is likely that the rich will become everything that someone longs to be, but without being willing to pay the price. Wealth is an image of what must be perfect, like the definition of God; many love it, but they sin every day with excessive practices, with everything that is not an image of the qualities coined to the concept of God, much less of the final meaning, wealth.

If in the long term you want to end up being rich, imitate the sense of good permanently. If we exemplify this idea, we will return to everything that has already been said. Meanwhile, practice prudence, perseverance, and all the other qualities that we have assigned to the authentic rich.

In the short and long term, the wealth is yours and is in you.

References

http://www.fao.org/economic/est/publicaciones/publicaciones-sobre-el-arroz/seguimiento-del-mercado-del-arroz-sma/es/

https://hbr.org/1979/09/risk-analysis-in-capital-investment

http://cmeluza-finmod.weebly.com/uploads/6/3/5/3/6353676/hertz_simul_hbr.pdf

http://www.infoarroz.org/portal/uploadfiles/20080212142543_9_analisis_del_mercado_mundial_de_arroz__patricio_mendez_del_villar.pdf

http://www.scielo.org.co/scielo.php?script=sci_arttext&pid=S0120-01352016000200002

https://www.portafolio.co/internacional/sector-arrocero-ee-uu-experimenta-cambio-estructural-134874

http://repositorio.utn.edu.ec/bitstream/123456789/1502/6/02%20ICA%20353%20capitulo%205%20II.pdf

http://economicas.unsa.edu.ar/afinan/informacion_general/book/7_SSRN-id986972.pdf

https://es.pngtree.com/element/down?id=MjAxNjUzMw==&type=1

www.ingramcontent.com/pod-product-compliance
Lightning Source LLC
Chambersburg PA
CBHW031943170526
45157CB00012B/1230